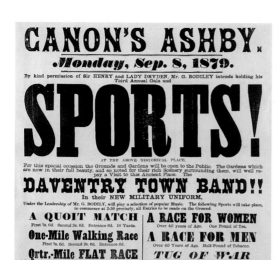

Canons Ashby

Northamptonshire

THE NATIONAL TRUST

'Antient as the Druids'

As you approach Canons Ashby through the rolling fields of this quiet corner of south Northamptonshire, the first thing that you see is the tower of the church. This is all that remains of the medieval priory of Augustinian canons from which Canons Ashby takes its name. North of the church is a hamlet that has barely grown since the 15th century. And right next to the road – not hidden away in its own park, like most country houses – is Canons Ashby itself.

More than a manor house, but less than a grand mansion, Canons Ashby perfectly reflects the character of the family who created and owned the place for four centuries. The Drydens were modest Northamptonshire squires – bookish, conservative-minded and often short of money. They remodelled and added to the building, but rarely swept away the past entirely, so that the fabric is now a fascinating and complex patchwork.

In 1551 JOHN DRYDEN inherited, through his wife, an L-shaped farmhouse (the present entrance range), which he gradually extended in a clockwise direction. He first added the staircase tower and the south-west block (now containing the Dining and Tapestry Rooms), and then about 1580 the Hall and Kitchen, to make a typical H-plan Elizabethan house.

In the 1590s his son, Sir ERASMUS DRYDEN, who bought himself a baronetcy, built the final, north range to enclose the Pebble Court. He decorated the Winter Parlour with the crests of his friends and neighbours, commissioned the obscure Biblical murals in Spenser's Room, and installed the vast two-tier chimneypiece in the Drawing Room. In the 1630s his son, Sir JOHN DRYDEN, 2nd Bt, added the towering ceiling plasterwork in the same room.

Between 1708 and 1717 EDWARD DRYDEN put up the smart classical panelling in the Dining Room, ordered new embroidered furniture, and laid out a formal terraced garden beneath the south front. But he was just as anxious to respect the antiquity of the place, medievalising the Great Hall with displays of weapons and heraldry, and proudly inserting in the Drawing Room overmantel the family motto 'Antient as the Druids'. Little has changed since his time.

The Victorian squire, Sir HENRY DRYDEN, was the most antiquarian of all the Drydens. He created the Book Room, where he amassed a huge library and archive on the history and antiquities of Canons Ashby and the county (now on deposit in the Northamptonshire Record Office and Northamptonshire Central Library). His daughter Alice began the tradition of photographing the house and garden, which was carried on by *Country Life* in 1904 and 1921. These images vividly record the benign neglect of Canons Ashby, as it gradually went to sleep during the early 20th century.

By the 1950s, however, decay increasingly threatened this extraordinary survival. In 1981, when the family generously gave the house, garden and church to the National Trust, they were all in a critical condition. A three-year restoration programme stabilised the fabric, revealed the decoration of the Winter Parlour, and revived the rare early 18th-century garden.

Sir Henry Dryden regularly opened the garden to visitors

(Right) The Kitchen in 1921

Tour of the House

The Entrance Range

You buy your ticket in the old coach-house, which was remodelled by Sir Henry Dryden in the late 19th century. The tea-room and shop were originally the stables, which were completely derelict when the National Trust acquired them.

Ahead of you, across the drive, is the modest east range, the central section of which is probably the oldest part of the house. Fifteenth-century cruck trusses in the roof suggest that it may have formed part of Wylkyns's Farm, which was already on the site when John Dryden arrived here in 1551 (see p. 34). Dryden adapted it as service quarters: to the right of the entrance door is the pump-room; to the left is the brew-house, where beer was brewed until the Second World War.

The gabled end wall of the wing at the far left (now containing Spenser's Room and the Painted Parlour) shows vivid evidence of how much the house has been altered over the centuries: at some point, a large opening on the ground floor was filled in, but the supporting beam remains embedded in the masonry; windows above have also been blocked up.

Walk through the passageway into the Pebble Court.

The Pebble Court

This central courtyard takes its name from the patterned cobbles with which it is paved. Looking clockwise from the entrance passage, it comprises: the brew-house; the Drawing Room range, with a massive protruding stack to take the flue for its huge fireplaces; the staircase tower (unusual in Northamptonshire); the west range, containing the 1½-storey Great Hall lit by tall windows, with the long and low gallery passage above, and the Kitchen in the right-hand corner; the north range contained the bake-house and laundry.

Originally, the Pebble Court would have been used only by servants hurrying between the service quarters in the east range and the Great Hall opposite. It became the main entrance to the house about 1840, when the Green Court (see p. 24) was grassed over by Sir Henry Dryden, who would have particularly appreciated the mellow, piecemeal quality of the courtyard stone and render. (Brick, which was more fashionable in the late 16th century, was reserved for the outside of the house.) The constantly changing courses of the rubble stonework, the sudden breaks in the masonry (for instance, at the left side of the tower), the oddly placed windows, the slightly haphazard way in which the Great Hall range abuts the tower – all testify to the complex way that the house has grown and been tinkered with. Old stone was also reused: for instance, the Tudor-arched Great Hall doorway may originally have belonged with the very similar doorways inside that room; and the little bull's-eye window may have been rescued from the priory ruins.

The Pebble Court, with the staircase tower on the left and the Hall range on the right

(Left) The Pebble Court around 1900; watercolour by Clara Dryden

The Kitchen

This was built as the kitchen for John Dryden's Elizabethan house in the cross-wing of his Hall range. Very unusually, it has remained the main kitchen ever since, the flagstones worn away by the comings and goings of generations of servants. As late as 1938 the only tap in the house was that over the Kitchen sink. It produced cold water, which had to be heated on the range before being carried in jugs by maids to the various bedrooms. Electricity did not finally arrive until 1947. According to Peter Dryden, recalling life in the late 1930s, 'The ex-maids all say the food was good and plentiful, but rather monotonous, so many rabbits in the winter, and a lot of mutton, for the Spanish and Jacob sheep were killed and eaten in the house.'

The *Victorian kitchen range* beneath the central arch was missing when the National Trust took on the house. It has been replaced by a similar, but slightly smaller, model. It would have been used for roasting meat in the ovens below and warming sauces on the hotplates. Set into the pier of the window wall is a stewing hearth, which would have been heated by charcoal or embers. To the left is a small bread oven. The high ceiling and the north-facing windows would have helped to keep the temperature bearable.

There was still no telephone in 1947. Internal communication relied on the servants' bells over the inner window and the speaking pipe, which once carried messages from the Dining Room at the opposite end of the building to the Butler's Pantry. The pipe now ends in the Kitchen; a hole in the wall reveals the original route.

The Kitchen

The sink and servants' bells in the Kitchen

The Dairy

This cool underground room made an ideal place for storing milk and cheese. It is now furnished with a late 19th-century oak barrel butter churn, a cast-iron cheese press and crocks.

Contents in 1717

A frame for cheesboard, 5 Bucketts, a chees-rack. An old chest, an old chair, 16 Chees-boards, 3 Tubbs. 5 Leads for Milk 2 Kettles, A brass pann, 11 Chees fastts. A Kever for Butter, Cheespress, 9 Milk pans, 2 Cream Potts, A churn, frame, 4 boards, A churn staff, 2 Trenchers, 2 Skimming dishes.

Return to the Kitchen and take the back stairs up to the Winter Parlour.

Furniture

The Kitchen contains replicas of two of the most important pieces of furniture once at Canons Ashby, a *circular oak table* of *c.*1600 and a *two-tier buffet* (sideboard) of *c.*1550. These rare Tudor pieces were probably relegated to the Kitchen after they had gone out of fashion, but were carefully recorded by Henry the Antiquary. They had disappeared by the time the house came to the Trust, but with the help of Henry's rubbings of their decoration, we were able to commission exact copies from local craftsmen.

The *colourful posters* on the wall by the exit door come from the vast family archive. Although the Drydens never aspired to lead the county, they were generous in opening the gardens for fêtes and galas.

Walk down the steps to look into into the Dairy.

The Dairy

The Winter Parlour

This room was created in the 1580s as a more private dining room for the family, who would have eaten in the Great Chamber (now the Drawing Room) only on special occasions. It was downgraded to a dining room for the upper servants about 1710, when Edward Dryden panelled the present Dining Room.

Decoration

The most extraordinary feature of this room is the decoration painted on the walnut panelling, which Trust conservators revealed under layers of later cream paint in the 1980s. Sir Erasmus Dryden probably commissioned the decoration in the 1590s to commemorate his ancestors and family connections. Strictly speaking, it is not heraldic, but features the crests and other devices of the Drydens, the families they married into, and important Northamptonshire neighbours, who may have been invited to Canons Ashby. Among the families represented are the Copes, the Staffords of Blatherwick, the Knightleys of Fawsley, the Fermors of Easton Neston, the Spencers of Badby and the Harbys of Adstone. The emblems are set in ovals within strapwork cartouches on a gold background, framed by jewellery-like motifs. Set squares and compasses appear on the panels around the recessed buffet, but these are unlikely to be masonic, as freemasonry did not become properly organised in England until 1717. In the frieze above are moralising Latin proverbs, which reflect Sir Erasmus's Puritan faith.

Furniture

The *18th-century oak gate-leg table* may be the 'large oval table' recorded in the Hall in 1717.

The panelling in the Winter Parlour is painted with the coats of arms of local families

The Winter Parlour

In the Lobby outside the Winter Parlour are a painting of one of the outdoor staff beside the Norwell spring (see p. 32), and one of Clara Dryden's watercolours showing Sir Alfred Dryden taking tea with one of his daughters in the Hall in 1911.

Cross the Hall to the Dining Room.

Proverbs

Imago animi sermo: 'Conversation is the mirror of the soul' (Seneca).

Lauda parce, vitupera parcius; illa siquidem adulatione, ista malignatate suspecta est: 'Praise sparingly, criticise more sparingly, or you will be accused either of flattery or malice.'

The Great Hall

This was the heart of the new house created by John Dryden, a place for festivities and greeting guests. You enter the Hall – as the servants would have done – at the 'lower' end, where a corridor, known as a screens passage, would originally have separated the room from the Kitchen and Buttery on the left. (You can still see the two blocked doors to these rooms in the right-hand wall.) Dryden and his visitors would have entered through a door at the opposite end of the passage: the recess is still visible. The flat ceiling was inserted at some point in the 17th century, when the walls either side of the fireplace were pushed outwards and the stone window mullions were introduced.

Edward Dryden blocked up the Tudor front door in 1708–10, when he inserted a grander entrance from his new Green Court in the centre of the outer wall. At the same time, he laid the floor of local Culworth and Byfield stone, removing a raised dais from the far end of the room. In the 19th century the Drydens played billiards in this room.

Furniture

In 1708 the room was very sparsely furnished with two old long tables and four benches. Shortly afterwards, the antiquarian-minded Edward Dryden decided to refurnish the room

The Hall in the 19th century, when it was used as a billiard room

The overmantel panel is painted with cannons, flags, drums and other weaponry

The *late 17th-century table* by the Green Court door has a top made from scagliola, a plaster composite that was coloured and polished to resemble marble.

Over the door on the south (left-hand) wall is a pair of large Jacob sheep horns. A herd of Jacob sheep was kept in the park from the 19th century until the Second World War.

Pass through the door by the Green Cloth to the Dining Room via the Stair Well.

as a medieval Great Hall with armour and heraldic decoration. Note the drawing and reproduction of a window catch incorporating the Dryden lion crest .

The *large overmantel painting*, probably by Elizabeth Creed, includes cannons, muskets and drums, together with elements from the Dryden and the royal coats of arms. Real weapons would originally have hung from the pegs, just as in medieval times, when entrance halls often served as armouries. The leather fire buckets have been here since at least 1717.

The *large green baize panel* is embroidered with the royal arms of William and Mary and belonged originally to the Board of Green Cloth, which policed the old Palace of Whitehall and still licenses pubs and theatres in this part of London. It probably came to Canons Ashby via Edward Dryden's brother-in-law, John Shaw, who was Master of the Board and may have received it as an office perk after Queen Mary's death in 1694.

The dummy board

This represents a Scots Guardsman and was painted between 1715, when the regiment was raised to counter the first Jacobite rebellion, and 1717, when the board was first recorded here. The artist was probably Elizabeth Creed, a Northamptonshire cousin of the Drydens, who also decorated the Painted Parlour and the church (see p. 16). Dummy boards are usually under life size, and so may have been designed to make a room seem larger than it actually was. They may also have been used simply to people an empty space or even to discourage burglars.

The Dining Room

Known by 1717 as the 'right hand parlour', this room was remodelled as a dining room around 1710 by Edward Dryden. He lowered the floor to give it more elegant proportions, and inserted the newly fashionable sash-windows. To make the room even grander and warmer, he also inserted the fine oak panelling with its fluted Corinthian pilasters.

In Victorian times, this was a convivial place: Henry the Antiquary's sole extravagance was a fondness for good claret. Using the speaking pipe to the right of the fireplace, he would have ordered up more bottles from the cellar. In the late 1930s, meals were still very traditional, as Peter Dryden remembered:

> Venison came to the table whenever deer were killed, the Drydens liked theirs hung to ripen, the maids ate theirs fresh. As far as possible the

(Right) The silver tea kettle is engraved with the coat of arms of Edward and Elizabeth Dryden

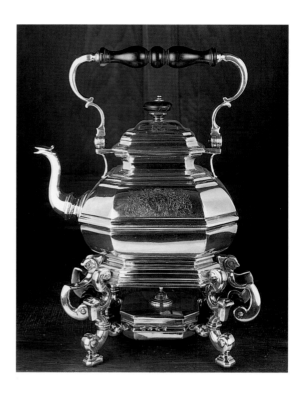

The poet John Dryden (1631–1700)

The greatest of all the Drydens, he was the uncle of Edward, who created this room, and his son would have inherited Canons Ashby, if he had not been a Catholic (see p. 38). Kneller possibly painted this famous portrait about 1698, when Dryden described himself as 'an old decrepid Man' to his cousin, Elizabeth Steward, with whom he often stayed at Cotterstock in the north of the county. It shows the poet finally laying down his literary laurels. Dryden's output was prolific and his range vast – from verse dramas, political satire and criticism to some of the finest translations of the Classics. He was appointed Poet Laureate in 1668.

There Dryden sits with modest smile,
The master of the middle style.

W. H. Auden

The Dining Room

household lived on their own produce, cows were kept to provide milk and butter; the pigs killed for bacon and hams, then the kitchen garden provided an abundant supply of all sorts of fruits and vegetables.

The *curtains* of scarlet moreen (a wool fabric imitating moiré silk) are replicas of those shown in the 1921 *Country Life* photographs.

Pictures

The best of the family portraits are here, hung oddly high under the cornice, just as the Drydens had them. They include Elizabeth Cornwallis (the mother-in-law of Edward Dryden), flamboyantly dressed as Diana the huntress in a portrait attributed to John Michael Wright. Two of her ancestors, Sir Frederick and Sir Thomas Cornwallis, flank the fireplace.

Left of the door is a portrait painted by William Staveley in 1795 of John Turner Dryden, 1st Bt, who inherited Canons Ashby in 1791. The previous occupant was Elizabeth Rooper, the 7th Baronet's second wife, whose portrait hangs over the sideboard.

Furniture and silver

The *walnut-framed mirror* over the fireplace was put up at the same time as the panelling, and was made specially to fit. The *dining-table* was possibly that bought by Sir John Dryden in 1753 from Vile & Cobb and, if so, is one of the plainest pieces produced by these fashionable London cabinetmakers. On the sideboard is a *silver tea kettle* and spirit burner made by Thomas Sadler in London in 1712 and engraved with the arms of Edward Dryden and his wife Elizabeth, perhaps to mark their wedding. Tea was still a very expensive commodity in the early 18th century.

The Staircase

The Staircase

The staircase tower probably dates from the 1560s, and seems originally to have contained tiers of living accommodation, with a much smaller spiral staircase in one corner, which still survives on the top two floors. In the early 17th century Sir Erasmus Dryden or his son Sir John built the present staircase, with its already old-fashioned 'grenade' finials and massive newel posts, to provide a grander route from the Hall to the first-floor Great Chamber (now called the Drawing Room). Over the years, it has been much altered to try to accommodate changes to the levels of the adjacent floors. Oddly, it now faces away from the Hall, and comes to an abrupt halt on the top landing. Extra steps also had to be added to link with the Tapestry Room.

The last tenant stripped the white paint from the woodwork and repainted it the present chocolate colour. The 19th-century heraldic stained glass in the landing windows records Dryden marriage alliances over 400 years.

Pictures and sculpture

The plaster bust on the ground floor to the right of the stairs is of John Dryden the poet. The marble original by Peter Scheemakers is in Poet's Corner in Westminster Abbey. On the first landing hangs a portrait of the Rev. Sir Henry Dryden, painted in 1818, the year he inherited Canons Ashby.

The Book Room

This room still powerfully evokes the character of its Victorian creator, Sir Henry Dryden the Antiquary, who never knowingly threw away a piece of paper. He christened the room (previously a billiard room), explaining that a library was where you borrowed books, while a book room was where you kept and read your own. He designed the neo-Gothic bookshelves and got the estate carpenters to build them in the 1840s and '50s. The cupboards at the bottom were used for storing garden tools as well as medieval manuscripts. (Sir Henry expected guests to help out in the garden.)

This part of the house was remodelled in the 1590s by Sir Erasmus Dryden, who installed the panelling. At a later stage he lowered the floor to allow room for the massive chimneypiece and overmantel. The carved oak coats of arms may have come from the old Cope house (see p. 33), as they represent the marriage of Sir John Cope (whose daughter married John Dryden in 1551) and Margaret Thame.

Books

Much of Henry the Antiquary's important collection of books, which included a First Folio of Shakespeare, was sold in the early 20th century, and the family papers are now deposited in the Northamptonshire Record Office. But about a quarter of the present library is indigenous, and includes a signed copy of Samuel Richardson's novel *Sir Charles Grandison* (1753–4), which is said to have been written at Canons Ashby. There are also early editions of Dryden and an important group of books by and about Isaak Walton, author of *The Compleat Angler* (1653), from the library of Marcus Stapleton Martin, who bequeathed Norbury Hall in Derbyshire to the National Trust.

Pictures

Between the windows is a pastel portrait of Elizabeth Creed, who painted the decoration in the Painted Parlour next door. The oil sketch to the left of the door to the Painted Parlour shows Henry the Antiquary in 1891 standing at the desk which he designed for his own use in 1849.

The Book Room

The Painted Parlour

Edward Dryden remodelled this room as a withdrawing room in the early 18th century. He seems to have commissioned his cousin, Elizabeth Creed, to produce its unique decorative scheme. This comprises fluted columns (painted to resemble marble), cut-out Corinthian capitals, a sloping frieze and decorative swags over the doors. Elizabeth would have been in her seventies and so may have turned to her daughter, Elizabeth Steward, who was also a gifted amateur decorative painter. The original sycamore floorboards were riddled with woodworm and have had to be replaced in the same wood. The gilt-framed mirror above the fireplace dates from Edward Dryden's time, but the marble surround seems to be an early 19th-century replacement. The early 18th-century cast-iron fireback may depict Queen Anne in her chariot.

Furniture

When Edward Dryden died in 1717, the room contained only brass firedogs, an ash shovel and 'tongues', and it is shown sparely furnished today, with the chairs pushed back against the walls, as they would have been in the 18th century. These *highback walnut chairs* were probably bought by Edward Dryden in London and are among the finest pieces in the house.

Retrace your steps through the Book Room and climb the stairs to the first floor.

Elizabeth Creed (1642–1728)

Elizabeth Pickering was a cousin of the poet Dryden and the diarist Samuel Pepys, in whose Navy Office her husband John Creed worked. She had eleven children, five of whom died in infancy, and it was only after her husband died in 1700 that she was able to start painting, providing free drawing classes for the local girls in Barnwell All Saints. She specialised in painting church monuments in a baroque style, complete with elegant epitaphs, the best being at St Mary's, Titchmarsh, in the north of the county. These include memorials to the poet Dryden and to her brother, the Rev. Theophilus Pickering, which cleverly combine sculpture with painted decoration of flowers, angels and symbols of death.

(Right) The Painted Parlour

The Drawing Room

This is the grandest room in the house, the Great Chamber of Elizabethan Canons Ashby, where important guests would have been entertained with food, music and dance. By the 18th century it had become the main family drawing room.

The room was considerably larger until 1710, when Edward Dryden refronted the south range and removed a large bay window, which spanned the three present sash-windows.

Chimneypiece

The massive fireplace and overmantel, which dominate the room, were commissioned by Sir Erasmus Dryden in the 1590s. Fantastic interlaced creatures ornament the underside of the mantelpiece and the frieze above. The Trust's conservators painstakingly revealed the rich original decoration under layers of later stone-coloured paint. The columns are marbled red, green and white, and the chimney surround is picked out in black and white to resemble marble and porphyry. The cornice is painted blue, red and gold. In 1710 Edward Dryden inserted the two central wooden panels painted with the family arms and a newly invented motto: 'Antient as the Druids'.

The fireplace had an Adam-style grate from the late 18th century until the mid-19th century, when Henry the Antiquary uncovered the original Tudor-arched lintel. Unfortunately, the chimneypiece seems to have started sagging alarmingly as a result, and Henry had to put in the present, rather awkward cast-iron columns to support it.

Plasterwork ceiling

Sir Erasmus's original ceiling was a simple barrel vault, the frame of which still survives in the roof-space above. Soon after Erasmus's son, Sir John, inherited in 1632, he decided to create a completely new domed ceiling within the existing vault. To support this, he had to thicken the walls, building them out into the room: hence the curious recess in which the chimney-piece now sits.

Sir John seems to have based his new plaster-work on the earlier scheme (fragments of which can be seen in the exhibition), as its style is somewhat old-fashioned for the 1630s. But it is still among the finest of its kind, featuring thistles and pomegranates and Indian princesses within strapwork cartouches. Above the fireplace Sir John inserted his own coat of arms, joined with those of his third wife, Honor Bevill, whom he married in 1632. A chandelier may originally have hung from the dramatic central pendant.

Furniture

The following pieces have been in this room since at least 1717: the two early 17th-century Flemish tapestries; the set of rare walnut chairs, c.1710; the carved walnut day-bed; and the *'seaweed' marquetry cabinet on chest*, c.1690, attributed to Gerrit Jensen, the Dutch-born royal cabinetmaker.

Pictures

These include watercolours of Canons Ashby in the 1890s by Clara Dryden, and a sketch of this room in 1963 by the neo-Georgian architect Prof. Albert Richardson.

The plasterwork ceiling features the heads of Indian princesses, pomegranates and thistles

The Drawing Room

Spenser's Room

This room is named after the poet Edmund Spenser (*c.*1552–99), author of *The Faerie Queene*, who was a first cousin by marriage of Sir Erasmus. According to the antiquary John Aubrey, Spenser visited Canons Ashby frequently and even had his own room here, but we do not know whether it was this one; Henry the Antiquary probably christened it.

Murals

This unique scheme was discovered behind early 18th-century panelling during the restoration of the house. It was probably painted for Sir Erasmus, as his arms appear on beams over a blocked-up bay window.

The grisaille paintings warn of the danger of worshipping false gods – a subject that would have appealed to a devout Protestant like Sir Erasmus, who may have used this room as his private study. They tell the story of Jeroboam from chapter 13 of the first Book of Kings. On the left, King Jeroboam is making a sacrifice at the altar of Bethel, when he is denounced by 'the man of God who came out of Judah'. Jeroboam's hand withers, after he orders the man of God to be seized. On the right, the man of God lies dead, having been killed by a lion, after having been tricked into accepting hospitality against divine instruction. In the background, his host rides out to recover the body, with 'the ass and the lion standing by the carcase'.

In the dado below is an interlaced geometric pattern in red, yellow and black. On the infilled door on the right is 18th-century graffiti of a parson and a fashionable lady.

Ceiling

The rococo decoration, which includes profile heads of the Four Seasons, was moulded in papier mâché, which was lighter and cheaper than traditional plaster. It was put up in the mid-18th century, when little other work was being done in the house. Papier-mâché decoration was popular in Northamptonshire country houses at the time.

Bed

The bed still has its 1830s valance, tester and headboard of red watered moreen. New bed-curtains were made in the same material, with window curtains to match.

Pictures

Over the fireplace is a portrait of Elizabeth Rooper, the second wife of Sir John Dryden, 7th Bt. They had no children, and so she ran Canons Ashby during her widowhood, from 1770 to 1791. There is another portrait of her in the Long Gallery painted by Joseph Highmore, whose most famous works depict scenes from Samuel Richardson's novel *Pamela*.

Retrace your steps back to the staircase landing and walk up the short flight of stairs opposite into the Tapestry Room.

The Tapestry Room

The Tapestry Room

This is the main first-floor room in the wing built on to the staircase tower by John Dryden in the 1560s. Originally, the fireplace was opposite where it is now, but the room was radically altered about 1710, when Edward Dryden was modernising the south front. He inserted three new sash-windows into the south (left-hand) wall, but because the floor level here is higher than in the rest of the range, he had to conceal the bottom half of the windows behind window seats to maintain the external symmetry. At the same time he covered up existing windows in the end walls and reused the existing 16th-century panelling. In 2000 the National Trust restored this arrangement in order to show the bed against the far wall, flanked by mid-17th-century Flemish tapestries. Unfortunately, not all of the original tapestries survived the 1960s, when a tenant used them as bedding for his dogs.

Furniture

Remarkably, the *suite of walnut furniture*, comprising six chairs, a fire-screen and a settee, still has its original early 18th-century embroidered covers, which show flowers in a Delftware pot, birds and pastoral scenes. Because they have always been kept under case-covers, they have retained their vivid colours. In 1716 Thomas Phill, upholsterer at the Sign of the Golden Chairs in the Strand, submitted his bill for the chairs, 'frames of ye newest fashion stufft up in Lynnen', and 'for makeing ye needle worke covers & fixeing ym on ye chaires'. They were sold in 1938 and bought back in

1983 with help from a generous benefactor and the Victoria and Albert Museum.

Sir Henry Dryden the Antiquary created the *oak four-poster bed* in the 19th century by reusing seven 16th-century panels. By the door is the chest in which Sir Henry kept his archive of material on Northamptonshire.

Return to the staircase landing and turn left up the steps to the Long Gallery, which is closed to visitors when the Dryden family is staying at Canons Ashby.

(Above) The settee in the Tapestry Room is covered with early 18th-century embroidery of pastoral scenes

The Long Gallery

This low corridor was probably created in the 17th century, when a floor was inserted over the Hall, which had previously filled the full height of the west range. It provided a link at first-floor level between the north and south ranges, but originally occupied the western side of the range and overlooked the Green Court. Perhaps because it opened directly into the Tapestry Room (where the doorway still survives), the arrangement was reversed: the old gallery was divided up into three rooms, and the present corridor formed looking inwards over the Pebble Court.

Pictures

The large group on the far wall is said to show Edward Dryden, who remodelled the house in 1708–10, with his wife Elizabeth Allen, and three of their children, but there is now considerable doubt about their identities. The other family portraits include one of Sir Alfred Dryden, painted by C. E. Butler in 1904.

(Left) A watercolour of the Gallery in the late 19th century by Clara Dryden

23

The West Front

This is the main façade of the H-shaped range, which John Dryden added to the staircase tower around the early 1580s. It served as the front entrance to the house until about 1840, when Sir Henry Dryden turfed over the Green Court. You would originally have entered the house through the little door on the left, which is decorated in the spandrels with the coats of arms of John Dryden and his wife, Elizabeth Cope. Like the north front facing the road, it was built in red brick with stone-mullioned windows, which still survive on the first and second floors of the right-hand wing.

In 1710 Edward Dryden blocked up the old doorway and replaced it with a new, grand and symmetrically placed front door, topped with a baroque cartouche in lead, which was probably made by John van Nost. Van Nost may also have supplied the elaborate rainwater heads, decorated with Edward Dryden's initials and the date 1708 (the year Edward inherited). His new drainpipes run straight across the old door, because this was not disinterred until the late 19th century. Edward also rendered the brickwork to match his new stone-faced south front (see p. 26), and inserted fashionable sash-windows on the ground floor of the flanking wings (those on the left, lighting the Winter Parlour, were filled in in the 19th century). He also added the wooden cupola, with its clock, to the Great Hall range. This was rebuilt by the National Trust in its correct form.

The Green Court

Edward Dryden planted this formal entrance court with topiary yew obelisks, which by 1981 had grown into unwieldy trees that overshadowed the garden and blocked the vista. So the Trust decided to prune them back to their original shape.

The *lead statue of a piping shepherd with a dog*, which originally stood outside the gates, is also attributed to John van Nost, who sent in a bill for £65 5s 10d in 1713. He mentioned further work for Edward Dryden on a gilded gladiator and 'a boy that I am making contrary to that you have'. The 1717 inventory lists 'a leaden Cupid painted white' and '2 Neptunes to throw water' (presumably garden fountains), which have not survived, but may also have been supplied by van Nost.

The gate-piers on the wall next to the Preston Capes road are topped by suits of armour, which were all part of Edward Dryden's antiquarian effort to emphasise the ancientness of his family. For the same reason, the gate-piers behind the van Nost statue support obelisks on S-scroll brackets. The remains of the oak gates were discovered beneath a mound of rubble in the burnt-out coach-house, and have been restored using as much of the original wood as possible.

The doorway into the main garden is probably 15th-century and may have been rescued by Edward Dryden from the ruins of the old priory.

The statue of a shepherd boy attributed to John van Nost stands in front of the early 18th-century gates of the Green Court

Henry the Antiquary's plan of the garden, showing the Green Court to the west of the house and the main formal garden to the south

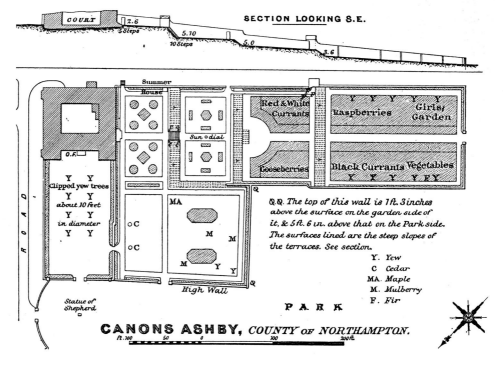

(Left) The west front and the Green Court

25

The Park

Avenues radiate out from the Green Court north-west across the deer-park, in which there is a medieval 'motte' (mound), planted with a clump of Wellingtonias. To the left of the main avenue is the pyramid roof of Park Cottage, which was built by Edward Dryden as a deer-larder, and enlarged about 1867 by Sir Henry Dryden to serve as a gamekeeper's cottage. (*It is not open to visitors.*)

In the 1840s Henry Dryden introduced a flock of the distinctive four-horned Jacob sheep to the park, which he acquired from a neighbour who had imported the breed from Spain. The flock continued to provide mutton for the table until the Second World War, and has recently been revived by the National Trust.

The South Front

This comprises three main elements. The five-bay block on the right may originally have been part of Wylkyns's farm (see p. 34). Sir Erasmus Dryden rebuilt it in the 1590s to take his new Great Chamber (now the Drawing Room), which originally had a large square two-storey bay-window projecting out from it. The central staircase tower was built in brick by John Dryden probably in the 1560s. On the left is the end of the H-shaped range that John added at the same time.

In 1710 Edward Dryden demolished the bay window, refaced the flanking blocks in the local orangey ironstone, and gave them a regular sequence of sash-windows. At the same time he rendered the tower to match the new stone

The south front

The garden in 1921, when the south front was partly hidden by four giant cedars

facing, and inserted the garden door on the ground floor.

Edward Dryden's alterations caused structural problems, which had become critical by 1981. The whole façade was bowing outwards and the massive Drawing Room ceiling was on the point of collapse. A major restoration campaign entailed pinning back the walls with an elaborate network of steel girders hidden in the roof. The render on the tower, last redone in hard cement in the 1930s, was also failing. It had to be completely renewed with a traditional mixture made from lime slaked in pits dug in the Home Paddock, and has now weathered down to a mellow buff colour. Craftsmen also remade the lead rainwater heads, following old drawings and what was left of the originals.

*The view from the south front down to the lion gates in
1921, when the rich Victorian planting was still kept up*

The Garden

Formal gardens probably surrounded the 16th-
century house, but all traces of them have long
since disappeared. What you see today was
mainly the work of Edward Dryden. Between
1708 and 1717 he created a formal garden of
axial paths and terraces, high stone walls and
grand gateways on the slope below the south
front in the then-fashionable style of the royal
gardeners George London and Henry Wise.
In 1711 the four terraces were called the 'best
garden', the 'upper garden', the 'lower garden'
and the 'little one below', and the main vista
connecting them was extended half a mile into
the park by a double avenue of elms. There
were also a Wilderness (an area of shrubs criss-
crossed by winding paths), canals (perhaps the
remains of medieval fish-ponds), an orchard

and a vineyard, which the Drydens may have
inherited from the priory. The gate-piers were
again decorated in antiquarian fashion – in this
case, with urns, smaller (and rarer) vases, and the
lion-and-globe crest of the Drydens. Edward
Dryden probably also installed the wooden
garden seats, to which timber canopies were
added about 1910.

It is typical of the conservative-minded
Drydens that they should have preserved this
design in the late 18th century, when so many
other owners were replacing such schemes with
acres of open grass in the style of 'Capability'
Brown. By the late 19th century, when Alice
Dryden took a series of romantic photographs
of the garden, the planting had matured, but
the yews were still kept clipped – with slightly
alarming consequences for visitors, as
J. A. Gotch recalled:

> The men of a house-party submitted to the
> process of hair-cutting, the operator being a
> versatile person who was at once postman,

barber, and the topiary artist who clipped the yews. Fortunately for his victims, the 'abhorred shears' which he used upon them were of a more delicate make than those he wielded on the trees.

By then, the rarity of the garden was increasingly recognised. Sir Henry Dryden opened the garden to the public, and provided a plan of it for Alicia Amherst's *A History of Gardening* (1895). It also appeared in H. Inigo Triggs's *Formal Gardens in England and Scotland* (1902) and in *Country Life* in 1904, becoming an important influence on the Arts and Crafts style of garden promoted by Sir Edwin Lutyens and Gertrude Jekyll.

The family continued to maintain the garden through the 1930s, when Bert Mood was employed to mow the lawns, using a machine drawn by a pony with leather shoes to prevent it from damaging the turf. In 1947 a gale brought down three of the four giant cedars planted around 1780, smashing the terrace steps. Over the next 30 years, the rest of the garden gradually disintegrated from lack of attention, and the elm avenue succumbed to Dutch Elm disease, so that the National Trust was faced with a huge task when it took over in 1981. However, a campaign of clearing and pruning revealed the bones of the original garden, which the Trust decided to reinstate because of its rarity. The terraces were laid out with formal plantings of Portugal laurels and 16th-century varieties of apples and pears. The steps were repaired and the four cedars replanted flanking them. In time, they will grow and once again hide the south front, which is meant to be seen from an angle rather than face-on. In 1990–1 a single lime avenue replaced the lost elms in the park, and another lime avenue now leads from the second terrace towards the church.

The National Trust is gradually re-creating the rare early 18th-century formal scheme

The Church

The pinnacled tower of St Mary's church is visible for miles around. This is only right as the story begins here. It was built about 1250 as the church of the Augustinian priory on the scale of a small cathedral. The Copes and the Drydens demolished the chancel, choir and half the nave, leaving only the two westernmost bays of the nave, which form the present church. The ground-level arcade of the west front (facing the road) comprises columns of the local dark orange ironstone which contrast attractively with the pale cream stone of the arches. The large Perpendicular window above was probably inserted in the late 14th century. Sir Robert Dryden rebuilt the south front in the late 17th century, and Sir Henry Dryden restored three of the tower pinnacles in 1838–57.

Interior

This tall, limewashed, barn-like space comprises the foreshortened nave and a single aisle from the priory church: hence its unusual proportions. The windows in the south and east walls were inserted in the 16th century. In the early 18th century Elizabeth Creed (see p. 16) almost certainly painted the baroque putti and curtains around the east window, which were revealed in the course of restoration. Sir Henry removed the coved ceiling and lowered the floor to what he thought had been the original level.

The west front of St Mary's church

Furnishings

Sir Henry rescued the 15th-century octagonal font from a nearby ditch, and in 1849 installed new pews in the traditional Anglican arrangement. Before then, the family had worshipped at a long pew placed against the south wall, facing their servants, who would have sat opposite in the faraway north aisle.

The Drydens are commemorated with almost every form of church monument: brasses, set in the floor, for John Dryden (d. 1584) and his son Sir Erasmus (d. 1632); on the south wall, Sir Robert's elaborate and old-fashioned funerary achievement, complete with helm and spurs (see p. 37); lozenge-shaped painted hatchments on the walls for the Dryden baronets and their wives, from Sir Robert (d. 1708) to Elizabeth Hutchinson (d. 1851); and Neo-classical wall monuments in white marble to Sir John Turner Dryden (d. 1797; by Charles Rossi) and his son, also Sir John (d. 1818). More modest wall tablets remember recent Drydens. To the left of the entrance door is a small circular plaque for the National Trust's Architectural Adviser, Gervase Jackson-Stops (d. 1995), 'who loved this place' and did so much to save it.

Restoration

Since the Dissolution of the Monasteries in the 1530s, the church has belonged to the owner of the big house and been outside the jurisdiction of the church authorities. This 'donative' status may have been what drew the Puritan Copes and Drydens to Canons Ashby in the first place. But it was also their responsibility to look after the building, especially as the congregation can never have been large. As the estate declined after the Second World War, so did the church, until it had to be boarded up to prevent vandalism. The National Trust took on this responsibility with the house, and with the help of a generous grant from the Department of the Environment brought the place back to life, reopening an old quarry at Stow-Nine-Churches to provide exactly the right kind of stone for repairing it.

The helmet, gauntlet, sword and spurs carried at Sir Robert Dryden's funeral in 1708 still hang in the barn-like interior of the church

Canons Ashby and the Drydens

The medieval priory

There are many Ashbys in Northamptonshire: the word simply means a farmstead. *Canons* Ashby takes its name from a group of canons who founded an Augustinian priory on a site to the south of the present church between 1147 and 1151. The Augustinians were a monastic order which came to England in the 12th century and were known as the Black Canons for their distinctive black habits. Their creed of poverty, celibacy and obedience became so popular that by 1350 there were over 200 separate small Augustinian communities in England: that at Canons Ashby probably never numbered more than thirteen. In 1253 they were granted a licence to build a well, and the little building, known as the Norwell, still stands in the field across the road from the house. Water was carried from here to the house in great hollowed-out tree trunks, which, astonishingly, remained in use until the 1920s. In the mid-13th century the canons also built the church, which would have been shared with the local community (see p. 30).

The village to the north of the house was never large, numbering 41 houses in 1343. Over the next century it shrank under the twin traumas of the Black Death (1348–52) and of enclosure, which drove many villagers from their land. The priory declined at the same time, and gained a somewhat dubious reputation as a stopping point for Oxford students, whose uncouth behaviour and slovenly dress provoked complaints. However, the last prior, Richard

Colles, was said to have been a learned and religious man. He certainly worshipped in some style in cloth of silver vestments, embroidered with fleur-de-lis and angels. In 1536 the priory was finally suppressed as part of the Dissolution of the Monasteries, and the following year was granted to Sir Francis Bryan, a close ally of Henry VIII who excelled at jousting and played a leading role in the christening of Prince Edward that year. But Bryan owned the estate for only a year, passing it on to Sir John Cope in 1538.

The Cope family

Sir John Cope was a wealthy Banbury lawyer, whose father had been a senior official in the household of Henry VII. In the late 16th century, the Copes were a prominent Puritan

The little building known as the Norwell protects a well first licensed in 1253. This anonymous 19th-century view of it hangs in the Lobby outside the Winter Parlour

The seal of the Augustinian priory was reproduced on a medal designed by Louis Osman, who lived at Canons Ashby in the 1970s (Goldsmiths Company)

The east front of the church, which is all that remains of the priory

family in the Midlands. John's brother, Sir Anthony, who was MP for Banbury, was imprisoned in the Tower of London in 1587 'for presenting to the Speaker a puritan revision of the common prayer book and a bill abrogating existing ecclesiastical laws'. Sir John may have been attracted here by the fact that the church lay outside diocesan control, and so allowed him to worship freely. He converted part of the monastic buildings into a house, which contained a hall, parlour, inner chamber and closet, nursery, armoury and gatehouse, all surrounded by a walled garden. Known as Copes Ashby, it survived until about 1665 in the ownership of the Cope family. The earthworks to the south-west of the church may be the remains of this building.

John Dryden (d. 1584)

Sir John Cope had sons and male cousins but, perhaps because they inherited property elsewhere, he was content to let the rest of his estate pass out of the family via his daughter, Elizabeth, who had married John Dryden in 1551.

The Drydens came from the faraway Cumberland village of Cumwhitton, eight miles south of Brampton in the foothills of the Pennines. The main branch of the family lived in the area until well into the 19th century.

By 1573 John Dryden had acquired the 'site of the late Monastery of Canons Ashby', retaining 'all such Glass, celings, tables, formes and tressells as were and doe remayne within the Mansion House of the said scyte of the said late Monastery and the wyndows of the same'. But he had already begun building himself a new house on a new site further north, which seems to have incorporated the farmhouse of Robert Wylkyns, the village carpenter. This 'Mansion House, lately Wylkyns farme', as it was described, probably comprised the central section of the south range of the present Canons Ashby. As money allowed, John Dryden seems to have gradually extended the building in a clockwise direction, adding the staircase tower and south-west block, which now contains the Dining Room and Tapestry Room, followed by the hall and kitchen ranges to create a symmetrical block with a typical Elizabethan H-shaped plan (see p. 4 for further details).

Sir Erasmus Dryden, 1st Bt (1553–1632)

John Dryden's second son Erasmus inherited Canons Ashby in 1584. He had probably been named after his uncle, Erasmus Cope, who would have succeeded to the estate if he had lived. The name also recalled the greatest of the Dutch Renaissance humanists, who was an important influence on Tudor Protestants like the Drydens. Indeed, Erasmus Dryden seems to have embraced the most extreme form of the faith, Puritanism. In 1604 he circulated a petition on behalf of local Puritans, for which

he was briefly imprisoned in the Fleet Prison in London. In 1608 he invited the charismatic Puritan preacher John Dod, who had been forbidden from preaching publicly, to become the family's chaplain, addressing him as 'our approved good friend'. Dod may also have played a part in bringing up the younger of Erasmus's six children, as he was the author of

RUBBING from a BRASS in the Church of Canons Ashby, Northamptonshire. John Dryden, temp. Eliz. Reg., ancestor of Sir Henry Dryden, Baronet, of that Ilk. Taken Sept. 24, 1817. J.C. Hutchinson.

one of the most influential Puritan guides to child-rearing, *A Godlie Forme of Household Gouernment* (1612).

Erasmus commissioned the murals in Spenser's Room, which tell the Old Testament story of the prophet Jeroboam. Dod would have interpreted these obscure images as a warning to the reformed clergy not to be taken in by Papists in disguise. The room takes its name from the poet Edmund Spenser, who was a cousin of Erasmus's wife, Frances Wilkes, and who is said to have often visited Canons Ashby. Erasmus also decorated the Winter Parlour with the emblems of his Northamptonshire neighbours and allies, whom he would have entertained in private in this room.

Erasmus's career as a prosperous grocer enabled him to afford a London house. In 1619 he bought himself a baronetcy for the large sum of £1,100, so that he would have the rank to serve as High Sheriff of Northamptonshire the following year. He also spent money on embellishing Canons Ashby, enclosing the Pebble Court with a new east range and installing the vast two-tier chimneypiece in his new Drawing Room.

Erasmus served as MP for Banbury in 1624–5, and found himself increasingly in conflict with the Crown. In September 1626 he was imprisoned once again for refusing to pay the forced loan demanded by Charles I. His grandson, the poet John Dryden, praised his actions in 'To my Honour'd Kinsman':

> … so tenacious of the Common Cause,
> As not to lend the King against his laws.
> And, in a lothsom Dungeon doom'd to lie,
> In Bonds retain'd his Birthright Liberty.
> And sham'd Oppression, till it set him free.

(Right)
A reconstruction of how John Dryden's H-shaped west range may have looked in the mid-16th century

(Left)
The tomb brass of John Dryden (d. 1584), the builder of Canons Ashby

Kitchen

steps

screens passage

Hall — dais

Parlour

Parlour

Sir John Dryden, 2nd Bt, commissioned the elaborate plasterwork ceiling in the Drawing Room, which is decorated with his coat of arms

Sir John Dryden, 2nd Bt
(1580–1658)

The 2nd Baronet was a Puritan, like his father, and is said to have been 'very furious against the clergy'. He was MP for Northamptonshire in 1640–53 and 1654–5, and, not surprisingly, supported the Parliamentary cause during the Civil War. In 1644 a party of Roundheads, who were quartered in the house, were driven into the church by a troop of Royalists from Banbury, and were finally forced to surrender when the tower, in which they had taken refuge, was set alight. The inside of the tower remains an empty shell to this day. An amusing pamphlet, issued as propaganda by the Royalists at the time, described how the mutton pies left out for the Parliamentarians by Lady Dryden on the wall between the Green Court and the road were devoured instead by the Cavaliers.

Sir John had succeeded to the estate in his fifties, and made only one major change, in the 1630s putting up the old-fashioned plasterwork ceiling in the Drawing Room, which prominently displays his arms with those of his third wife, Honor Bevill.

Sir John's daughter, also called Honor, received flattering letters from her cousin, the poet John Dryden, who as a young man in the 1650s often came over from his parents' house at Titchmarsh in the north of the county. But if there was a romance, nothing came of it.

The much-faded and damaged mural in the family flat may show an interior in Sir John's time. It includes an early depiction of a wall-clock

Sir Robert Dryden, 3rd Bt (d. 1708)

In 1658 Sir Robert inherited Canons Ashby, which was to be his home for the next half-century. He demolished the old Cope mansion around 1665, but seems to have done very little to the main house, although as late as 1819 there was still a room named after him. He never married, and he seems not to have got on with his poet cousin, who never visited Canons Ashby during his years of fame, preferring the Huntingdonshire branch of the family. The inventory taken on his death in 1708 gives a good idea of how the house would have looked in his day. The Hall was sparsely furnished with only '2 old long Tables & 4 Forms'; the 'Best Parlor' had '4 little Tables & 2 Carpitts, a Skreen & 12 old Turky worke Chairs, som broken, 2 Arm & 6 other Cane Chairs/ a pr. Brass andirons, 1 old Carpitt'. Very few of his possessions survive at Canons Ashby.

Sir Robert's funeral in 1708 was a grand affair. The arch at the west end of the church had to be cut away to allow room for his funeral catafalque to be brought inside. He was buried like a medieval knight with a full funerary achievement – banner, helmet with the Dryden lion and sphere crest, tabard, sword, shield, gauntlets and spurs – which still hang in the church. The funeral was paid for by his heir, Edward Dryden, who had good reason to be generous, as he was not the obvious choice.

Edward Dryden (d. 1717)

Sir Robert's eldest cousin, John, became the fourth Dryden baronet, but did not inherit Canons Ashby, perhaps because he had displeased him by marrying the daughter of the 2nd Baronet's steward, Edward Luck. The next in line was the poet's son, Erasmus Henry, but he was a Catholic, and laws passed in the late 17th century penalised Catholics inheriting property. So Sir Robert decided to leave Canons Ashby to the poet's nephew, Edward Dryden, who was not only a Protestant, but also wealthy enough to support the estate, thanks to a rich wife and to his prosperous grocery business at the sign of the Pestle and Mortar in King Street, Westminster. Edward's London house was in Bolton Street off Piccadilly, which in 1708 was the westernmost street in the capital.

Edward Dryden was to own Canons Ashby for only nine years, but in that time he made the

(Left)
Edward Dryden
inserted his coat of
arms into the
Drawing Room
overmantel

(Right)
The suite of
embroidered chairs
in the Tapestry
Room was bought
by Edward Dryden
in 1716 from
Thomas Phill, a
London upholsterer

(Left)
Edward Dryden's
sister, Mary;
attributed to
Michael Dahl
(Tapestry Room)

first major changes to the house for 80 years.
He tried to impose a baroque symmetry on the
rambling Tudor exterior by inserting a new
central doorcase in the west front, with a florid
cartouche above, and by remodelling the south
front with more fashionable sash-windows; this
entailed a certain amount of juggling inside to
make them align. He also commissioned a new
formal garden of descending terraces in the style
of the royal gardeners London and Wise, which
was enclosed by high stone walls with obelisk
gate-piers. Inside the house, he lowered the

floor of the Dining Room to give his new
panelling the correct classical proportions. He
also bought new furniture from the best London
makers, much of which is still in the house.
But Edward was just as anxious to acknowledge
the long history of the house and of his family.
The first in a succession of antiquarian Drydens,
he decorated the Hall with arms and armour in
mock medieval style, and he coined a new
family motto, 'Antient as the Druids', which was
inscribed on new heraldic panels in the Drawing
Room overmantel.

The 18th and early 19th centuries

Edward's eldest son, Sir John Dryden, 7th Bt, put up the papier-mâché ceiling decoration in Spenser's Room, but otherwise Canons Ashby seems to have escaped Georgian modernisation almost entirely. Among his visitors was the novelist Samuel Richardson, who is said to have written much of *Sir Charles Grandison* here. In the novel, the Northamptonshire home of the heroine is called Ashby-Canons, and a presentation copy survives in the Book Room, inscribed on 18 April 1758: 'Given to me today by the hands of Mr Richardson that worthy friend his own Self.' Sir John had no children, and so on his death in 1770 the house was retained by his widow, Elizabeth, who lived on here quietly for another 21 years.

The estate then passed to Sir John's niece Elizabeth, who had married Sir John Turner from the Oxfordshire village of Ambrosden 25 miles to the south. Turner, who was the son of a prosperous London merchant and chairman of the East India Company, took the Dryden name and in 1795 had the Dryden baronetcy revived for himself. In his youth he had made the Grand Tour of Europe and, despite being a badly-off second son, gained a reputation as a spendthrift, who 'shone in convivial circles'. He was commissioned into the Foot Guards, and, according to one contemporary, 'became one of the most fashionable young men about town; in short, he dissipated a large sum of money'. But before he could run through the whole of his new inheritance, he died of asthma aged 45 in 1797.

(Right, top) Sir John Dryden, 7th Bt, who owned Canons Ashby from 1717 to 1770, but did little to the house (Dining Room)

(Right) Elizabeth Rooper, the second wife of Sir John Dryden, 7th Bt. She lived on at Canons Ashby as a widow until 1791; by Joseph Highmore (Long Gallery)

Sir John's eldest son inherited young, and died young and unmarried in 1818, leaving Canons Ashby to his younger brother. Like many younger sons of the gentry, Henry had entered the church, but he still lived on a grand scale and had a wife, also called Elizabeth, with even more expensive tastes, which considerably exceeded the estate's annual income of £3,000. She kept a pack of hounds at Canons Ashby, which were commemorated in verse by her son Leopold:

> In the first place there's Dark, who looks
>   wondrous wise,
> In the next there is Carlo with rather
>   weak eyes.

The Rev. Sir Henry Dryden had antiquarian interests, excavating round the church to reveal the extent of the medieval priory. In 1829 he also commissioned William Litchfield of Daventry to survey Canons Ashby with the intention of remodelling the east front with a central oriel window over the entrance. A mound of cut stone was gathered, but perhaps because money was running short, the work was never carried out. A serious, fussy and somewhat feckless man, he found himself continually in debt, and being harassed by unpaid tradesmen.

In the 1830s, before the railway arrived, Canons Ashby was still very inaccessible. The roads were bad and not yet fenced, so that one had to open and shut 25 gates on the first six miles of the ride to Banbury.

(Right, top) Sir John Turner Dryden, 1st Bt, who inherited Canons Ashby through his wife Elizabeth in 1791, but died young in 1797, the year this portrait by William Staveley was painted (Dining Room)

(Right) The Rev. Sir Henry Dryden, 3rd Bt, who owned Canons Ashby from 1818 to 1837 (Staircase Landing)

Sir Henry Dryden 'the Antiquary' (1818–99)

He succeeded his father in 1837 at the age of nineteen and was to be master of Canons Ashby for almost the entire Victorian era. He inherited his father's antiquarian interests, which embraced local history, archaeology, medieval architecture and Celtic runes. He was nick-named 'the Antiquary' as a result. The Northamptonshire architect J. A. Gotch, who was befriended by him as a young man, remembered his 'genial personality, his indefatigable researches and his quaint and sometimes unconventional observations'. A High Tory, he liked to describe himself as the last of the Black Canons. In the 1880s he was still wearing the Regency dress of his youth: white canvas trousers, a yellow check waistcoat and a stock or loose cravat round his neck. For his long walks over the estate, he wore a shabby Norfolk jacket with baggy pockets and a forage cap, and was sometimes taken for a tramp. He would invite travellers he encountered on his walks back to Canons Ashby, where they would be entertained in the ancient kitchen with a glass of his home-brewed beer – a mixed pleasure, as it contained bicarbonate of soda. According to an obituary, his 'income was small, but he was quite free from meanness'.

At school, Henry's headmaster had reported that he 'didn't at all shine in academic subjects, but he was good at drawing'. He became an accomplished architectural draughtsman, producing thousands of measured drawings of Canons Ashby and other historic buildings in the county, together with rubbings of decorative details. (These proved invaluable when the National Trust was restoring the house.) He was also fascinated by the Celtic history of the Orkneys and Shetlands, publishing an illustrated history of St Magnus Cathedral, Kirkwall.

Henry was the first owner since the 18th century to live at Canons Ashby all year round, but he had neither the inclination nor the money to modernise the antiquated heating and other services. So he made do with a four-seater earth-closet in the Pebble Court and in 1844 abandoned plans for a large new stable block, preferring to remodel two existing buildings for his horses. His other changes were also in keeping with the ancient character of the place. He reinstated the old mullion windows in the east front, and having grassed over the Green Court, brought visitors in through the old Pebble Court. Appropriately, the only room he altered inside was the Book Room, in which he wrote a stream of pamphlets at a desk he had designed himself. These included one modestly entitled *On Mistakes concerning Architecture*

Canons Ashby, photographed by Alice Dryden in 1886

Sir Henry Dryden the Antiquary in the garden with his wife Fanny and their only child Alice

committed by Myself. But in fact the new cottages and barns he built on the estate, which are marked 'HD', showed a sympathy for setting, local material and vernacular tradition that was rare in the Victorian period.

In 1865 Sir Henry married Fanny Tredcroft. He was 47; she was 42. This late, happy marriage produced only one child, Alice. When she was born, Henry complained, 'There are too many women in the house already', and promptly sacked two kitchenmaids (who were quietly reinstated by his wife). Although Alice received little formal education, she was brought up to share her father's interests. As a birthday present he gave her a camera, which became her favourite hobby. Despite being partly paralysed by childhood polio, she drove herself about in her dog-cart, making a systematic survey of the local buildings and their inhabitants. Her mother had been a keen patron of the Northamptonshire lace industry, and Alice revised Mrs Palliser's classic *History of Lace* in 1902. Her friend, the Northamptonshire historian Joan Wake, recalled 'her high intelligence, entertaining conversation, her sometimes caustic humour, and keen interest in the present as well as the past'. She was a typical Dryden.

Alfred Dryden taking tea in the Hall in 1911; watercolour by his daughter Clara

The 20th century

Sir Henry's brother Alfred succeeded to the estate in 1899 at the age of 78. He was then a retired barrister living in Putney and initially he stayed at Canons Ashby only in the summer. However, around 1904, when the house was first photographed by *Country Life*, he decided to settle permanently in Northamptonshire. In 1906 Gotch renewed the render on the tower and the north front, and made essential repairs inside, including mending the cracked cornice in the Drawing Room. Sir Alfred was a knowledgeable botanist and enthusiastic planter of trees. Until his late eighties he was often to be seen walking briskly across his land or working in the garden.

His son, Sir Arthur, was also an energetic London lawyer, who would often bicycle the 70 miles to Canons Ashby. He again inherited late in life, when he was confined to a wheelchair. He added the late 17th-century-style wrought-iron gates, but otherwise made very few changes. He was content to live a quiet bachelor existence, being looked after by his two unmarried sisters, Clara and Mary, and a small number of long-serving and devoted servants. Queen Mary paid a visit in 1937, attracted by the house's atmosphere of romantic decay. She found that it still had no proper plumbing or electricity.

Between 1937 and 1938 Sir Arthur, his only brother and two of his sisters all died. His sole surviving sister Louisa and her only surviving son, Cecil Pritchard, found themselves inheriting the entire estate. Cecil had joined the Indian army before the First World War, in which both of his brothers had been killed. After the war he qualified as a chartered accountant before emigrating to Southern Rhodesia in 1926. Louisa lived in Liphook, using Canons Ashby only in the summer, as she found the place intolerably cold in winter. The house was mothballed during the Second World War, when it was looked after by the chauffeur, Albert Mold, and the chief parlour-maid, Ada Moring. Electricity and modern plumbing were finally installed in the late 1940s, but after much heart-searching, Cecil Dryden (as he became) decided to let the house, because family and business commitments kept him in Africa for the greater part of the year. His three sons were also settled there.

From 1962 Canons Ashby was rented by a faith-healer, Dr Christopher Woodard, and his brother Peter, who made heroic efforts to restore the house, which was by then in a very dilapidated condition. The next tenant was Louis Osman, a man of many talents, who had trained as an architect and restored Staunton Harold church in Leicestershire for the National Trust. His greatest achievements were as a goldsmith. He set up a workshop at Canons Ashby, where he created the crown used for the investiture of the Prince of Wales in Caernarfon Castle in 1969 and a gold and enamel casket to celebrate the US Bicentennial in 1976 – two of the most important pieces of 20th-century British metalwork. He was devoted to Canons Ashby, but got into financial difficulties with his business and had to give up the tenancy.

By 1980, the house was in a parlous state. The north range was riddled with dry rot, and the garden front was bowing outwards, threatening to bring down the tower and the Drawing Room ceiling. The roofs leaked and the garden had run to seed. The family, still resident in Africa, did not have the financial resources to undertake a full restoration of the house. It was decided to let the house unfurnished, so the Drydens retained the smaller items of furniture and all the portraits and made arrangements for the sale of the remaining furniture and the books by public auction. Meanwhile, the land agents were actively seeking prospective tenants who could meet the terms of a full repairing lease. Tentative negotiations were in hand to let the house as a residential conference centre, when the National Trust began to take an interest.

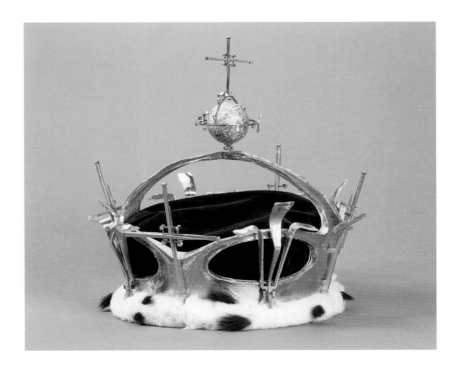

The investiture crown of the Prince of Wales, which was made at Canons Ashby in 1969 by Louis Osman

The National Trust

The Drydens had first opened negotiations with the National Trust in 1937, but nothing came of them. As a schoolboy in the 1960s, Gervase Jackson-Stops, the Trust's Architectural Adviser and a native of Northamptonshire, had cycled past the house. He was now determined to save it. With the generous help of Simon Sainsbury's Monument Trust, he managed to rescue much of the more important furniture when it was sold in July 1980. He then persuaded the family that the newly founded National Heritage Memorial Fund offered a way of saving the house and maintaining the link with the family. The NHMF gave £1 million to provide an endowment, together with £500,000 towards the cost of repairs. The Landmark Trust (which created a holiday flat in the tower), the Historic Buildings Council, the Department of the Environment, the Victoria and Albert Museum and a public appeal all made vital contributions towards the rescue effort. In return, the Drydens very generously gave the house, garden, outbuildings, church and land to the National Trust in 1981, together with the proceeds from the sale of the Woodyard Barn near the church. Most of the portraits and many of the chattels in the house are on loan from the family.

A comprehensive three-year restoration programme, led by Rodney Melville, followed. A steel frame was inserted into the roof of the Drawing Room to save the sagging plasterwork ceiling. The unique painted decoration in the Winter Parlour was painstakingly revealed from under layers of cream paint, and the important suite of embroidered chairs was returned to the Tapestry Room in 1983, again with the help of the Monument Trust. The family retains a flat in the house, and today has closer links with the place than for 70 years. Against considerable odds, Canons Ashby has survived the 20th century with its fragile atmosphere of calm intact.

Repairing the dangerously sagging Drawing Room ceiling in 1981

FAMILY TREE

Owners of Canons Ashby
are shown in CAPITALS

Asterisk denotes a
portrait on show

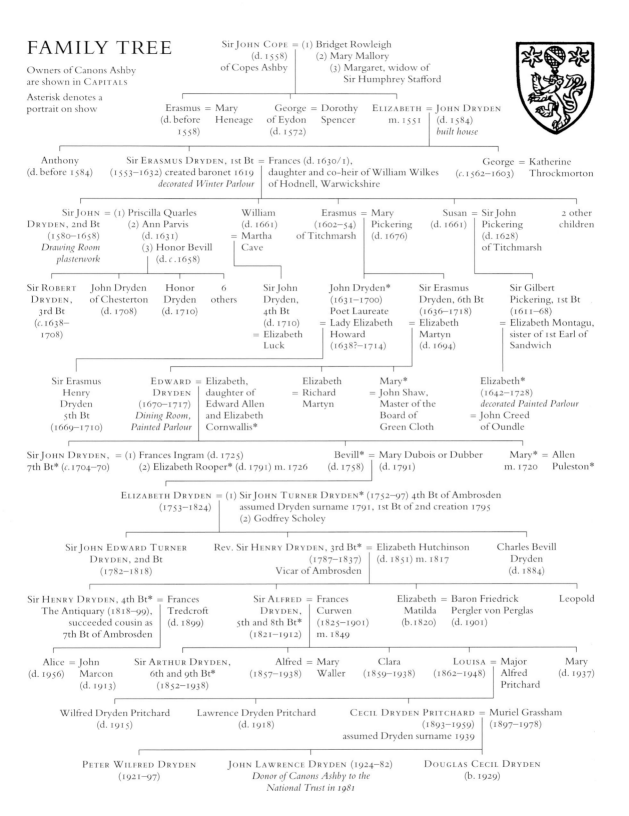

Sir JOHN COPE = (1) Bridget Rowleigh
(d. 1558)   (2) Mary Mallory
of Copes Ashby   (3) Margaret, widow of
Sir Humphrey Stafford

Erasmus = Mary   George = Dorothy   ELIZABETH = JOHN DRYDEN
(d. before   Heneage   of Eydon   Spencer   m. 1551   (d. 1584)
1558)   (d. 1572)   *built house*

Anthony   Sir ERASMUS DRYDEN, 1st Bt = Frances (d. 1630/1),   George = Katherine
(d. before 1584)   (1553–1632) created baronet 1619   daughter and co-heir of William Wilkes   (c.1562–1603)   Throckmorton
     decorated Winter Parlour   of Hodnell, Warwickshire

Sir JOHN = (1) Priscilla Quarles   William   Erasmus = Mary   Susan = Sir John   2 other
DRYDEN, 2nd Bt   (2) Ann Parvis   (d. 1661)   (1602–54)   Pickering   (d. 1661)   Pickering   children
(1580–1658)   (d. 1631)   = Martha   of Titchmarsh   (d. 1676)   (d. 1628)
Drawing Room   (3) Honor Bevill   Cave   of Titchmarsh
plasterwork   (d. c.1658)

Sir ROBERT   John Dryden   Honor   6   Sir John   John Dryden*   Sir Erasmus   Sir Gilbert
DRYDEN,   of Chesterton   Dryden   others   Dryden,   (1631–1700)   Dryden, 6th Bt   Pickering, 1st Bt
3rd Bt   (d. 1708)   (d. 1710)   4th Bt,   Poet Laureate   (1636–1718)   (1611–68)
(c.1638–   (d. 1710)   = Lady Elizabeth   = Elizabeth   = Elizabeth Montagu,
1708)   = Elizabeth   Howard   Martyn   sister of 1st Earl of
                     Luck   (1638?–1714)   (d. 1694)   Sandwich

Sir Erasmus   EDWARD = Elizabeth,   Elizabeth   Mary*   Elizabeth*
Henry   DRYDEN   daughter of   = Richard   = John Shaw,   (1642–1728)
Dryden   (1670–1717)   Edward Allen   Martyn   Master of the   *decorated Painted Parlour*
5th Bt   *Dining Room,*   and Elizabeth   Board of   = John Creed
(1669–1710)   *Painted Parlour*   Cornwallis*   Green Cloth   of Oundle

Sir JOHN DRYDEN, = (1) Frances Ingram (d. 1725)   Bevill* = Mary Dubois or Dubber   Mary* = Allen
7th Bt* (c.1704–70)   (2) Elizabeth Rooper* (d. 1791) m. 1726   (d. 1758)   (d. 1791)   m. 1720   Puleston*

ELIZABETH DRYDEN = (1) Sir JOHN TURNER DRYDEN* (1752–97) 4th Bt of Ambrosden
(1753–1824)   assumed Dryden surname 1791, 1st Bt of 2nd creation 1795
               (2) Godfrey Scholey

Sir JOHN EDWARD TURNER   Rev. Sir HENRY DRYDEN, 3rd Bt* = Elizabeth Hutchinson   Charles Bevill
DRYDEN, 2nd Bt   (1787–1837)   (d. 1851) m. 1817   Dryden
(1782–1818)   Vicar of Ambrosden   (d. 1884)

Sir HENRY DRYDEN, 4th Bt* = Frances   Sir ALFRED = Frances   Elizabeth = Baron Friedrick   Leopold
The Antiquary (1818–99),   Tredcroft   DRYDEN,   Curwen   Matilda   Pergler von Perglas
succeeded cousin as   (d. 1899)   5th and 8th Bt*   (1825–1901)   (b.1820)   (d. 1901)
7th Bt of Ambrosden   (1821–1912)   m. 1849

Alice = John   Sir ARTHUR DRYDEN,   Alfred = Mary   Clara   LOUISA = Major   Mary
(d. 1956)   Marcon   6th and 9th Bt*   (1857–1938)   Waller   (1859–1938)   (1862–1948)   Alfred   (d. 1937)
      (d. 1913)   (1852–1938)   Pritchard

Wilfred Dryden Pritchard   Lawrence Dryden Pritchard   CECIL DRYDEN PRITCHARD = Muriel Grassham
(d. 1915)   (d. 1918)   (1893–1959)   (1897–1978)
                                                 assumed Dryden surname 1939

PETER WILFRED DRYDEN   JOHN LAWRENCE DRYDEN (1924–82)   DOUGLAS CECIL DRYDEN
(1921–97)   *Donor of Canons Ashby to the*   (b. 1929)
                 National Trust in 1981

Bibliography

The extensive Dryden papers are deposited in the Northamptonshire Record Office; they include a large number of drawings by Sir Henry Dryden the Antiquary. Some material on Canons Ashby can also be found among his archaeological collections, bequeathed to Northampton Central Library.

ALDINGTON, Araminta, *A History of the Jacob Sheep*, Geerings, 1991, pp. 43–7.

ANON., 'Canons Ashby', *Country Life*, 31 December 1904, p. 978.

BAKER, G., *The History and Antiquities of the County of Northampton*, 1822–41, ii, pp. 4–17.

BARRON, Oswald, ed., *Northamptonshire Families*, Victoria County History, London, 1906, i, pp. 43–5.

BRIDGES, J., *The History and Antiquities of Northamptonshire*, 1791, i, pp. 223–30.

CORNFORTH, John, 'Canons Ashby', *Country Life*, 9, 16 April 1981, pp. 930–3, 1026–9.

CORNFORTH, John, 'Canons Ashby revisited', *Country Life*, 28 June, 5 July 1984, pp. 1856–60, 20–4.

CROFT-MURRAY, Edward, *Decorative Painting in England*, 1962, i, pp. 68, 247, 259 [on Elizabeth Creed and Elizabeth Steward].

COOPER, Nicholas, *Houses of the Gentry 1480–1680*, Yale University Press, 1999.

GOTCH, J.A., 'Canons Ashby', *Country Life*, 26 February, 5, 12 March 1921, pp. 246–52, 278–84, 306–14.

GOTCH, J.A., *The Old Halls and Manor Houses of Northamptonshire*, 1936, pp. 84–6.

HEWARD, John, and TAYLOR, Robert, *The Country Houses of Northamptonshire*, Royal Commission on the Historical Monuments of England, 1996, pp. 114–26.

JACKSON-STOPS, Gervase, 'A Set of Furniture by Thomas Phill at Canons Ashby', *Furniture History*, xxi, 1985, pp. 217–18.

KASEY MARKS, Sylvia, 'Literary Associations: Canons Ashby and Samuel Richardson', *Northamptonshire Past and Present*, vii, 1989, pp. 343–5.

SARGANT, David, *Sir Henry Dryden of Canons Ashby*, Northamptonshire, Delapre Books, 1993.

SARGANT, David, 'Sir Henry Dryden, Baronet (1818–1899): A Centenary Tribute', *Northamptonshire Past and Present*, 52, 1999, pp. 85–7.

TAYLOR, S.J., 'An Excavation on the Site of the Augustinian Priory, Canons Ashby', *Northamptonshire Archaeology*, ix, 1974, pp. 57–64.

VICTORIA COUNTY HISTORY, *Northamptonshire*, 1906, ii,1, pp. 130–3 [on priory].

WATERSON, Merlin, *The National Trust: The First Hundred Years*, National Trust, 1994, pp. 204–8.

WINN, James Anderson, *John Dryden and his World*, Yale University Press, 1987.

WAKE, Joan, 'Alice Dryden', *Northamptonshire Past and Present*, ii, 1956, pp. 157–9.

Sir Henry Dryden the Antiquary at the desk he designed for himself in the Book Room